Ask Jackie

Canning Basics

Copyright 1999-2012
ISBN: 978-0-9860152-1-2

Backwoods Home Publications

Edited by Jessie Denning, Julia Denning, Haley Kessel,
Connie Sayler, Lisa Nourse, Rhoda Denning, and Ilene Duffy
Cover art by Don Childers
Illustrations by Don Childers, Jessie Denning, and John Dean

Contents

Introduction   5

Canning basics   7

Pressure canning   23

Water bath canning   50

Lids and jars   57

Storage   73

More canning questions   79

Introduction

Canning is one of those life skills that kind of fell by the wayside. Luckily, a lot of independent-thinking people are again discovering how fun and easy canning is. No matter where you live, you can easily learn to can a great deal of your own food quickly and inexpensively. Not only is this home canned food great tasting and free of any chemicals or preservatives, but it will last on your pantry shelves for decades, remaining fresh and nutritious right in those beautiful jars lining your pantry.

To can safely, it is essential to have proper equipment for the type of food you are going to can, along with a good canning book. You can often find good used equipment such as: water bath canners for canning fruits, jams, jellies, preserves and pickles; pressure canners for low-acid foods like vegetables and meats; and boxes of canning jars at yard sales and estate auctions. I've even found some for free!

I began my own foray into canning as a young girl "helping" my grandmother and my mom can in our basement in Detroit. It's always been a part of my life and I'm so glad I learned the basics at a young age so I could put them to use every year, through all the seasons. It's such a wonderful skill to learn.

In this book I answer questions about canning basics, water bath canning, pressure canning, jar lids and types of jars, and storage of home canned foods, along with a whole lot of miscellaneous questions.

Enjoy reading. I hope I've managed to answer many of your own questions too! **— Jackie Clay**

Ask Jackie

Canning basics

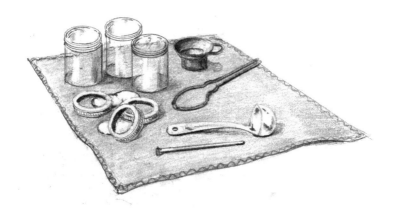

Canning book for beginners

I am getting interested in canning, but having no previous experience, I need a good place to start. I have an old book printed in 1956 that details canning methods, but is it sufficient for modern-day canning methods? If not, can you recommend a good book or two on the subject? A basic search on Amazon.com yields dozens of possibilities and is somewhat overwhelming for a novice like me.

Lana Flavies, Massachusetts

I wouldn't recommend a 1956 canning book. There have been some changes since then. For instance, there are now low-acid tomatoes that weren't around back then. And some practices that were previously thought of as "safe" have been proven unsafe.

7

A good, easy-to-read, cheap canning manual is the *Ball Blue Book Guide to Preserving*. It is a paperback and available at most local hardware stores and even Wal-Mart.

I promise you'll love canning your own food. It is so easy and the foods taste so much better than store-bought foods do. Especially if you can what you raise yourself! It's always so exciting to me, even after canning for more than forty years, to pick a mess of beans and have them canning merrily in only half an hour. Now that's fresh!

A few basic canning questions

I purchased an All-American pressure canner online and have a few interesting questions. Inside my pressure canner I have this thin round disk made of aluminum and was wondering. Inside a pressure canner do I just put the jars on the bottom of the canner, or do I put the metal disk on the bottom?

My next question is simple also: how does one double stack canning jars; is it okay to just put jars on top of one another?

Lastly, does anyone know where to get the pressure gauge tested? I've asked everyone I know and most people don't even know what a pressure canner is let alone where to get the gauge tested.

Chris Deere, Canada

The round disk is to put on the bottom of the canner to keep the jars from resting directly on the bottom of the canner, which quite often makes them break from direct exposure to the heat. (Actually, the bottom breaks out of the jars.) You just drop the disk in, add water, then warm it up and add your jars. So simple they don't tell you. (Hey, it took me a day to figure out how to put the paper into my word processor!)

To double stack the jars, you need another separation between the layers of jars. I use a cut down grill rack I got at the dollar store. It fits nicely inside my canner and has many rings of heavy wire, set close together so the jars rest on it and it allows the steam to circulate freely around and under the jars.

You can usually get your pressure gauge tested at your Extension Office. This is most often located at the courthouse at your county seat. If they don't do it there, they probably can send it out for testing. It's a simple test and only takes a few minutes. And it's usually free!

Learning to can foods

I'm starting to try to learn to can stuff; got a water bath canner from Shetler's and jars and lids. I thought there would be a book of some kind with it, but there wasn't. I have been retired for 5½ years and got a fair garden and orchard going. I can't see things going to waste. Could you give me a few instructions and some times to boil things like peas, green beans, corn and such, especially tomatoes and juice?

Charlie Coss, Ohio

Good for you, Charlie! Sounds like you're off and running. But to keep you going, please don't try to process vegetables and meat products in your water bath canner. Boiling does not kill deadly bacteria that can invade your jars. To kill them, you must use steam generated by a pressure canner. The foods that you are able to can in your new water bath canner are many: tomatoes, fruit and tomato juice, jams, jellies, pickles, fruit, and even milk.

You can buy a good, inexpensive canning manual, such as the *Ball Blue Book*, at most stores that carry canning equipment. Even Wal-Mart sells it.

In the meantime, you can go to your library and borrow a canning manual or book. If they don't have one on the shelves, they can get one from inter-library loan. You can then write down notes to tide you over until you get your manual.

Don't try to can without one. I open one for every food I can, and I've been doing it for more than 40 years.

You can also look at a few back issues of *BHM* and pick up times and instructions on many foods from my articles and this column.

Canning with aspirin is neither safe nor effective

Do you know about canning apples with aspirin? I have put up rhubarb with ice water and it works just fine.

Nellie Jacobs, Alaska

Canning with aspirin was a fad for a while. It is not a safe or effective way of canning. You should always follow the simple water bath steps to put up both apples and rhubarb so you won't have moldy or unsafe fruit later on.

Canning safety

I love your column and your common sense practical advice. But I do have a question: I recently took classes (from the cooperative extension program) to become a "master food preserver" in California. We were taught that it is unsafe to can thick "butters" like pumpkin because the heat distribution in the center of the jars is uneven. Wouldn't that apply to things like canned bologna as well?

I also recently heard that the USDA has stopped recommending drying your own jerky (without boiling the meat first which makes it yucky) due to bacterial problems. I have found most of what you say to be exactly what I was taught. My mom canned for years, many times with methods not "approved" and never had a problem, but since you are giving public advice, many times to novices, maybe you should err on the side of caution? Or do you have info that hasn't reached California yet?

JD, California

No, I'm not smarter than Californians, especially those with initials following their names. Today it's the trend to keep us safer from ourselves. The reason for the latest canning bans on dense foods is that it is possible that people do not process their food long enough, thus not heating it in the center. This is the reason that most raw meat is "exhausted" or heated before being placed in a canner.

Many times learned folk caution home canners on things that could possibly happen, not what actually does happen in real life. I have never heard of a person becoming sick from eating home canned pumpkin butter or bologna. And while it is possible for you to pick up bacteria from home dried raw jerky, it is also possible for you to pick up bacteria from restaurant food or the play yard at McDonald's. You cannot be totally safe in life. Period.

I try to give a mixture of common sense and scientific fact in my column, and do try to "err on the side of caution," but it seems that every day someone decides that something I do is no longer safe, from riding a horse to canning bologna. I am not perfect, only a very experienced old homesteader.

Old canned goods safe?

I lost my home due to fire back in October of 2007. I had quite a big pantry, and saved some of the store bought canned food and bottles of apple sauce. Just in case they might still be good. Some of the cans have light surface rust; most all the labels are mildewed. On top of that they have been in an unheated shed since October with temperatures ranging from 18°F to 65°F currently. I just wondered if these items would be safe to eat, if I gave them a good bath in chlorine water, and remove the rust and labels. Any thoughts would be greatly appreciated.

Chris Childers, North Carolina

I'm so sorry to hear about your fire. Mom and Dad also had a bad house fire many years back. Luckily, Mom, too was able to save most of her large pantry full of both store bought and home canned foods. These are usually fine to eat; safe as long as the cans remain intact or jar seals remain sealed. On occasion, some foods will have softened because of freezing. This may damage the texture, but will not affect the safety of the food. As with any canned food, look at the can or jar before you open it. Cans with bulges should be tossed. Any food that looks yucky, smells bad, or has mold should also be thrown out. In reality, most of the food will probably be edible and fine.

You will have an interesting time trying to find out what those label-less cans are, though! It'll make for some interesting dining. The best of luck recovering from your fire.

When it's necessary to can

I have a question on the canning process. My sister-in-law and I are questioning when it's necessary to "can" (i.e.: hot water bath or pressure can) all foods? We have seen some books say that jars can be placed upside down for a time or just skip the hot water bath process altogether, and the jars will still seal. If the food is already cooked, is the hot water bath or pressure canning necessary?

Carol Weber

While there are a few high-acid foods that will be okay and seal when the foods (jams, pickles, jellies, etc.) are put hot into hot sterilized jars in small batches, most foods require some type of processing to be safe. Just because the food has been cooked, it is not heated hot enough to have killed bacteria and molds which can make food spoil.

Generally speaking, for your foods to be safe and to seal dependably, follow the directions of a good, fairly recent canning book and don't wing it too much. All low-acid foods, such as meats, vegetables, and mixes thereof, must be pressure canned to be safe to store and then later eat.

Boiling home canned foods

I have always seen specific instructions to be sure to boil home canned vegetables for a certain number of minutes before using or even tasting them. Is it necessary to boil home canned meats and soup stocks before using them?

Ruth Marvin, Washington

Yes, it is recommended that we bring canned vegetables and meats up to boiling temperature and hold them there for 10-15 minutes, just to be sure that any possible bacteria is killed. This can be done in the oven, on the stovetop, or by frying.

Canning times

I just took up canning. How does one find the process time for a recipe? I want to pressure can a purée of bell peppers, hot peppers, celery, and garlic that is great in chili.

John Sargent, Michigan

When you are new to canning, it's best to use "tried and true" recipes for a while. Then when you get the knack of it, and understand the whys and wherefores, you can home can your own recipes, taking care to process the recipe for the time needed for the ingredient with the longest processing requirement. In this case, the garlic is (I would guess) a spice and not too much is used. The peppers are processed for 35 minutes, celery for 30 minutes, so your half-pints or pints would process for 35 minutes at 10 pounds pressure, providing you live at an altitude of 1,000 feet or less above sea level. If you live at a higher altitude, consult your canning manual for directions on adjusting your pressure.

Greasy liquid in canner

I got brave after reading your wonderful article in the March/April 2008 issue titled "Canning meals in a jar." I tried the shredded barbecued beef, the chicken noodle soup, and the meatballs in sauce. All came out well and the family loves it. However, I am just baffled about how the jars seal. I go to great effort to fill the jars with a funnel and wipe the rims well before applying the hot seals. Then during the canning process the liquid gets out into the canner and leaves greasy water. If greasy liquid is coming out of the jar, why am I cleaning the rim in the first place? Sorry, I just don't get it!

Nancy Murray, Tennessee

You clean the ring first of all to check again for nicks in the glass, secondly to remove any pieces of food that might prevent sealing, and finally to remove grease from the rim of the jar. Yes, greasy liquid sometimes oozes out of the jar, between the lid and the rim, during pressure canning. This happens most often with foods containing meat because of the long processing required. And yes, sometimes you have a jar or two that doesn't seal, because the grease of a tiny bit of food has gotten between the lid and rim. But this happens much less than you'd think, all things considered. And it certainly doesn't happen often enough to make me hesitant to can my handy, dandy meals in a jar!

Keep wiping those rims. And enjoy your good meals.

"Hot seal" canning question

How safe is the "hot seal" canning method for preserving barbecue sauce? I'm cooking my sauce over 170 degrees for about an hour and boiling my lids. Most of the sauce doesn't last more than 2-3 weeks before being consumed by family and friends.

The sauce has a lot of sugar, vinegar, and ketchup in it — no tomatoes.

Gary Hairlson

Your method of canning your barbecue sauce is probably just fine. Without seeing your recipe I can't be positive, but I wouldn't be afraid to take second helpings. The sugar, vinegar, and ketchup (which does have tomatoes, obviously, but also sugar and vinegar to preserve it) would not cause food poisoning or mold problems.

Canning problems

I have canned pickles, and during the water bath process the lids pop up ¾ of the way through the boiling process. I gradually bring the water up to temperature and let the jars simmer for 10 minutes. The seal usually seals tightly, but on occasion the seal does not happen. What can I do? I am getting ready to can corn. Can you help me with this?

John Small

The best way to ensure a good seal while water bath canning is to use hot foods, in hot jars, placed in a very hot water bath canner full of water, then bring the whole shebang up to a rolling boil quickly. Time the processing, then immediately remove the jars to a dry, draft-free place, leaving several inches between the jars so they cool down relatively quickly.

When you can corn, you must use a pressure canner because corn and other vegetables are low-acid and must be pressure canned for safety. When you remove your jars from the canner, again be sure they have some room around each jar and I'm quite certain you'll have good seals. (Be sure to wipe the rims of the jars clean. It only takes a tiny amount of food on the rim to cause a seal to fail.) I'm sure you're following your canning book's directions to the T, as well.

My canner won't seal

I was trying to can some fish and my pressure cooker won't seal. I don't know any other way to store it. Can you help me please?

Patty

I'm hoping that you are canning your fish in a pressure canner, as a pressure cooker really isn't meant for canning. Usually when the canner won't seal it means that the rubber seal in the lid has become stiff. Almost any good hardware store that carries home canning equipment and supplies can sell you a new seal. This is inexpensive and a quick fix for your problem.

However, sometimes the canner has become pitted or developed a nick or crack. This is not repairable and you must replace the unit.

In the meantime, you can freeze the fish in small packs until your canner is back working again. To test it before you use it again, just bring it up to pressure with no jars inside — only the required water. If it comes up to pressure with no leaking, you're back in business.

Ball and Kerr canning lids

I have a complaint that I would like addressed in your forum. Ball and Kerr are owned by the same company. They no longer use rubber around the inside of the lid from what I have been told by the company. It is a synthetic product. For the last few years I have called them and complained. They send a form to fill out, listing all kinds of reasons why my jars didn't seal. I have been canning for over 30 years and know exactly why a jar didn't seal. Now I am being told that I should let my jars sit for 24 hours. By that time the food is not fit to eat and if I reprocess it right away, I end up with mush. I am so angry about this I could scream. I feel sorry for new canners who find that their jars don't seal and are convinced that it was something that they did. It sure would discourage me from trying again. All of that time and money wasted.

My main problem is with pressure canned foods. The lids seem to seal well in a hot water bath. They will also seal if I leave the jars in the pressure canner overnight without opening it. There is a definite problem here. I am losing four or five quarts out of seven. The old lids were so forgiving.

Please address this problem.

Colleen Mysliwiec

Colleen, I really sympathize with all your troubles. As canning is such a huge part of our self-reliant lifestyle, I can imagine how frustrated you must be. Two years back, I also had trouble with Kerr lids, but the problem was a crease which formed in the lid after pressure canning chiefly meats and poultry which require longer processing time. But the lids did seal, albeit peculiarly.

I've canned hundreds and hundreds of jars in the past few years and can truthfully say that I've not had more than about one percent that did not seal. I'm not thrilled that Ball and Kerr are now owned by the same company, but I don't blame the lids on your failure, though I can sure see why you would. But let's see what could be happening.

I had a bunch of quarts of cold packed, pressure canned sweet corn that didn't seal once. I was literally canning a pickup full of corn and was in a real hurry, using two canners, going 24 hours a day. And I was in too much of a hurry.

I didn't let my canners get hot enough, after putting all those jars of cold corn in them. When steam sputtered out the exhaust vents, I shut them and went on. Not good enough. The vents should have had a steady stream of steam exhausting before they were closed. The canner simply didn't get hot enough, even with the pressure built up. Subsequently, the jars sealed poorly. Even some that appeared to seal later spoiled when the seal broke during storage. It was a big lesson for me.

A good friend had trouble with her jars not sealing. I went to her house during canning to find out why. Everything went great until she went about wiping the film off the jar lids while they were still hot. A big no-no. The jars need to be left totally alone until cool to the touch. When she did this, every jar sealed fine.

I would check the gasket on your canner, if it has one, to make sure it is pliable and not cracked. Also have the gauge checked, if your canner has one instead of the jiggling weights. I'd strongly suspect that something was wrong with the pressure during processing, caused by a faulty gasket or pressure gauge, as you don't seem to have any problems with water bath canning.

Another thought: you're not "helping" the pressure return to zero by manually letting off a little pressure are you? I've been tempted to do this a couple of times when I was in a dead hurry to get the jars out of the canner and had a few jars not seal. They can also break if you do this.

Still another way a few friends have caused jars not to seal is to retighten rings after processing. This often breaks the seal already in place. They thought that because the rings seemed loose, and the directions said "complete the seal," that this was what they should do. It sounds reasonable, but that "complete the seal" is for old-fashioned lids and rubbers, and just confuses things today when few folks use them.

I know this may seem banal, but let's go through the basics in pressure canning. It might help someone who has not canned much and may strike a chord with you. (Some of us who have canned for years occasionally take shortcuts and ax ourselves by doing so.)

• Fill clean jars with prepared food, according to directions. Wipe the rim with a moist, clean cloth.
• Place the boiled lid in place.
• Screw ring down snugly, without force.
• Place jars in canner.
• Tighten down lid evenly all around.
• With petcocks open, turn on heat.
• When steam exhausts steadily, close petcocks.
• When pressure builds to desired pressure, begin timing.
• Keep heat even, adjusting minutely to keep at desired pressure.
• When time is up, turn off heat and wait till pressure returns to zero.
• Carefully open petcock to release any remaining steam.
• Open the canner and remove the jars at once to a clean, dry place, out of drafts, padded with a folded dry towel.
• Leave alone until cool, then wash and remove rings.
• Store in cool, dark, dry place.

I'm really sympathetic towards your problems. If you can't resolve them, let me know and I'll call you and see if we can't work this out. I want you happily canning.

Recanning products

My husband passed away Dec. 17, 2009 (tick bite). I can all the fruits, vegetables, jellies, etc. I would like to know if I can buy large jars of sauces, BBQ, salsa, and spaghetti, and recan them in half-pints, as I can't eat a large jar. It molds in the fridge so I use a water bath or pressure cooker to recan these. I am 78 years old and your column makes my life fun, as you are so down to earth. I have 10 acres here. I have no water in my place. I have an outside pump. Good ole faithful two seater. I do all my work, even repair my tractor, mowers, and anything that needs tender care. I lived and taught school in Alaska 47 years. I lived in a one room cabin, drank Yukon river water, lived off the land mostly, ordered store boughten things once a year from Fairbanks, which came down the Yukon once a year on a barge. Boy, what fun. Like a child, especially the fruit juices, which nine out of ten times were missing. Our fridge was a hole back under our bunk bed; about nine inches down was solid ice and outside, the same. We had a larger hole about four feet deep for moose, beaver, porkies, etc. I canned a lot; anything I could get my hands on. We smoked sometimes a thousand fish. We packed them in waxed boxes and stored them up in our cache about 10-12 feet above ground. All our goodies were stored there also. We sold our fish Jan. Feb. for $23 lb.

Our old cabin was 47 miles from the nearest person, we named it "Willi-Waw 2." We had an old 14-foot wooden boat with a 25 H.P. motor. We were almost killed many times trying to get to Russian Mission or Holy Cross. We loved it. Still do. I would love to take my husband's ashes back and spread them on the mountain in back of our cabin. I am writing a book (trying to) about our 47 years in my dear Alaska. I am alone, but keep busy. It's lonely without Delton.

Eileen Widener, Minnesota

You sound like you've had a really great life so far. Remember, there's still the "end of the book" so don't quit looking ahead, too! We never know what joys are lurking around the corner. I want a copy of your book! Remember me.

Yes, you can recan those large cans (#10) of tomato sauce, spaghetti sauce, etc. I've done it a lot, especially when we didn't have a huge tomato crop and #10 cans were cheap. Some foods don't recan well, as the food softens a lot, but fruits, tomato sauce, cheese sauce, and some pickles/pickled peppers do can up nicely into manageable-sized jars.

Pressure canning

Safe canning

All of Jackie Clay's articles always say you must use a pressure canner. Me and my wife have been canning meat, vegetables, jam, you name it and have never used a pressure canner. We have canned food sitting on the shelves from three years ago that Jackie says you must pressure cook. I have hams and bacon hanging in the smoke house that I will can this fall. I can deer meat and sausage patties, and cantaloupe. No pressure canner. Now I know Jackie is a good writer and I love her articles. Is she afraid of liability or was she just never told the Amish or old way?

Michael Ettinger, Pennsylvania

You bet I know the old Amish (and other old-timer) way. Would I can meat, vegetables, and poultry without a pressure canner? *No way!* Jam, pickles, tomato products, fruit, and other high-acid foods, of course.

No, I'm not afraid of being sued. I'm deadly afraid that one of my cherished readers might eat a jar of green beans, venison, or whatever, that is seasoned with botulism toxin. It is not a common thing, especially if you boil your food for 15 minutes before you eat it, but it can kill you or one of your children.

Many of my Amish friends use a pressure canner, as well as the good old water bath for fruit and high-acid foods. It only makes good sense. There is no reason not to use the pressure canner. It is not expensive, especially if you buy a good used one. It is easy to use. It works well. And it home cans food safely.

(Just because you've never had a house fire, would you let your kids play with matches?)

Pressure can or water bath?

My question: is there any reason why you couldn't use the pressure canner to do tomatoes, pickled beets, or any of the fruits or vegetables that would normally be done in the water bath? I love the pressure canner since I learned how to do it! It's really so much easier than water bath to me. A friend of mine always did her produce in the pressure canner, but couldn't remember how many minutes for pints or quarts.

Tammy Amland, Minnesota

You can do tomatoes in a pressure canner, but not pickles or fruits because the temperature is too high and they would become real mushy. All vegetables must be canned in a pressure canner. Always. I see no benefit to doing tomatoes in a pressure canner as you must constantly monitor the pressure canner while it is processing, while you can do something else once your boiling water bath canner is boiling and you've begun counting your processing time. But if you wish to use it, you certainly can. For tomatoes, you would process pints and quarts at 10 pounds pressure (unless you live at an altitude above 1,000 feet and must adjust your pressure to suit your altitude; consult your canning book for directions if necessary) for 10 minutes (packed in boiling water) or 25 minutes (packed in their own juice).

Pressure canning

I just read with interest your article "Canning 101." In it you talk about all the different things you can at home. I am just starting out with canning ... never tried it before and I do not have a pressure canner. I do have a pressure cooker but understand it cannot be used for canning. I've been searching high and low for some simple recipes for canning fish, rabbit, bear, moose, meatballs, stews, etc. But every recipe requires a pressure canner. Is there a way of taking one of these recipes and converting it so I can use my regular canner? If I could follow a recipe but know how full to fill the canner and how long to process, it would be great.

Kimberley Pierce

Sorry, Kim, but it is absolutely necessary to use a pressure canner to home can all meats, fish, poultry, and vegetables. I know a pressure canner is expensive when bought new, but it will last you for a lifetime. You are looking at about $120 here if you get one new, or you can usually find a good used one by advertising for one or shopping at yard sales, thrift stores, or the Salvation Army. I bought a good second canner for $5 last year, complete with the manual and several canning tools. I'm sure if you really try, you can do just as well. I would advise having the pressure gauge checked by your home extension office to be sure it is accurate. Just to be sure.

I am always for the easiest, safest, and cheapest methods of doing everything. But I also won't save money when the cost may be a poor job or my family's health. Pick up a pressure canner and discover how many wonderful foods you can put up at home. It's easy. And it's safe.

Smaller canner

What size pressure canner do you use?

Since I haven't canned for more than 20 years, I'm getting ready to purchase a new canner (probably an All-American). However, as I'm getting older, I don't necessarily want to get the biggest and heaviest.

Also, since I have a glass stove top (dumb selection!), I'll need to get a stand alone propane burner for it. Does that need to be a single or double burner? I'm also presuming I should only use it outside?

Sally, California

I'm not getting any younger either, Sally. While I still have the huge canner I've used for years and years, it does weigh nearly 30 pounds empty. So when I thought I'd pick up another canner to have on hand, I got a smaller one. And I find that does fine on most smaller canning jobs and it's a lot lighter! Mine is an All-American 921. It will hold seven quarts or 19 pint jars.

I'd advise getting a two-burner propane burner as they are more stable under a full canner's weight. You can use this on an old table right in your kitchen. Some even come with legs so they can be used anywhere. When I was a child, Mom and Grandma canned on one in the basement because it was much cooler down there in the hot summer.

Pressure canner advice

I am looking into buying a pressure canner and would like your input as to whether the weighted type or the gauged type is better. Thanks.

Matt Stone, New York

I much prefer the pressure canners with a gauge over the weighted types. In that way, you can see exactly what is going on — before it happens and surprises you. But both types work fine. Mom has used a weighted jiggly vent canner for years and years. And who do you suppose taught me to can?

Pressure canning and peeling tomatoes

I would like to purchase a pressure canner and learn to can. I was wondering what brand and model of pressure canner you use. I plan to grow some tomatoes this year and those will be my first attempt at canning. I think that I have read in the magazine that canned tomatoes should be peeled. Is there a particular reason to peel them? I am not bothered by tomatoes that have the skins on them.

Ron Szczepanski

My old canner is really not a "canner" at all. Let me explain. Twenty-seven years ago, my former husband and I were at a State Hospital auction and there was a brand new, huge autoclave, used for sterilizing surgical instruments and bandages. Now an old autoclave is nothing but a very large pressure canner, so I bought it for $50. It holds seven or eight quarts and eighteen pints all at the same time. It, like me, is getting a bit old, but it still performs very well. But it weighs a ton. I have two smaller pressure canners picked up at yard sales, a National and a Presto. Both work fine, but require replacement of the ring gasket from time to time.

I plan on buying a new canner this year, through Lehman's — their #921, which holds 7 quarts or 19 pints and costs $159. This is a smaller version of my huge monster, having no gasket (steel to steel) and having a pressure gauge. As I only have one child home, instead of eight, my canning needs are much less. I also have a bad back (no, not from my homesteading, from an old accident), so lifting a 40-pound empty canner onto and off the stove is getting old.

While you can use your pressure canner to do tomatoes, you can more easily use a water bath canner — those big, blue enameled kettles with a cover and inner rack.

Tomatoes are extremely easy to can, and therefore make a perfect "first try" at canning. The reason you peel the tomatoes is that the canned peels are pretty tough and tend to roll up into unpalatable straw-like pieces. Tomatoes are real easy to peel. Just drop a few into a kettle of boiling water and boil about a minute. Then fish them out with a slotted spoon and plunk them into a sinkful of cold water. The skins split and slip right off; no real peeling to it. Then if you make salsa or tomato sauce, you have no tough peels to deal with.

Pressure canner manual

I bought a used pressure canner, and have replaced all gaskets, etc. that needed replacing. I have been unable to locate an instruction book for it. Here are the specifications: 16 quart, model number 0406, Mirro pressure canner, 15 lb. weighted gauge.

Julia Rader, Arkansas

PickYourOwn.org is a website that has downloadable instruction manuals for the Mirro pressure canner. This is a very standard canner and most any canning book with pressure canning instructions will tell you how to use it.

Basically, add 2 inches of water to the bottom, put in the rack, add your filled jars, and seal down the lid without the weight on it. Then turn on the heat and let the canner exhaust steam for 10 minutes, counting from when steam is flowing out in a steady stream. Put on the weight and let it build pressure. At 15 pounds, the weight will jiggle about 4 times a minute to maintain the pressure. Turn down the heat if it jiggles a lot more than that to maintain the pressure. When the processing time is done, turn off the heat and let the canner cool down.

To see if the pressure is down to zero, gently nudge the weight with a spoon handle. If spurts of steam come out, let it cool more. If none comes, remove the weight and open the lid to remove the jars.

Pressure canning

When canning in a pressure cooker, what if the water level is ¾ of the way up the jar? Does that affect the pressure in the product of the jar? I canned this way for years. I also run my canner one pound over in order to protect the product. I have it tested yearly though. I've canned since I was 10 years old. I now teach my 10 year old grandson and 14 year old granddaughter. Some day they may need to teach this to others.

Vicki Hildebrandt, Kansas

It would be better to only have two inches or so in your canner, as a lot of extra water creates extra steam. I don't know if it would affect the pressure, but most canner manuals advise us to use only two inches. It's fine to run your canner a pound over pressure, but it's not necessary if your canner is tested yearly. Higher than necessary pressures can soften some foods such as carrots and potatoes, so I try to hold mine at the correct pressure for our altitude.

I'm so glad that you are teaching your grandchildren to can. You are passing on a valuable skill. So many moms and grandmothers did not do this, and now a whole generation has to learn to can from scratch. Good for you!

Pressure gauge

Last year I purchased a 23-quart Presto pressure cooker/canner and had some concerns about how to properly affix the pressure gauge and relief valve. My dad, being a millwright, suggested that I put Teflon tape on the threads to make it seal better and easier to come off during maintenance or cleaning. I was wondering if this would compromise the canner in any way.

Adam Browne, Canada

No, using the Teflon tape won't damage the integrity of the seal. He's right, it'll make it easier to get off later on.

Pressure canning with a weighted regulator

I use a 22-quart pressure canner by Mirro, which uses a 3-piece weighted pressure regulator. A lot of the canning literature I've read warns if the pressure drops below the recommended pressure setting, to raise it and start your process over from the beginning. Without a dial gauge, how can I be assured I'm maintaining the correct pressure consistently? Would you recommend a canner with a pressure gauge instead of weights? I'm a bit bored canning the same published recipes over and over again, and prefer to can my own soups and stews. Can I use the soup ingredient with the longest process time to determine the total processing time of the soup? For example, potatoes might be 40 minutes at 10 lbs., while beans are 20 minutes at 10 lbs. And soup stock is 25 minutes at the same weight. By combining them, can I process everything for 40 minutes?

Michelle Graceffa, California

There are pros and cons for each type of pressure regulator. The weighted regulator is noisy as it spits and spurts out small bursts of steam to maintain the pressure. It can only regulate the pressure in 5 pound increments; 5 pounds, 10 pounds and 15 pounds. So if you need to can your food at 12 pounds pressure, you must can it at 15 pounds. Ten pounds is not enough and the 15 pounds is a little higher than necessary, but it's your only option.

But the weighted regulator is accurate and doesn't need to be periodically tested as does a dial gauge to make sure it is reading correctly. You can lose the weight, but it'd be extremely hard to damage it. The dial gauge is silent and you can regulate the pressure minutely. But you do have to stand nearby during processing because it sometimes creeps too far up or slides too far down and you must stop that by increasing or decreasing the heat as needed.

With the weighted regulator, you want it to spit out regular small bursts of steam. If it isn't spurting steam several times a minute, you need to raise the heat a little. If it is spurting steam frequently, you need to reduce the heat. The pressure remains at the setting on the weight, regardless.

Personally, I prefer the dial gauge because I can regulate the pressure more easily and not over-process food.

I home can my own recipes all the time, but you must read your ingredient list carefully and have a full understanding of basic canning principles in order to be safe. For instance, if you have a recipe that has tomatoes, beans, onions, corn, and spices, you may **not** use a water bath canner because it has a tomato base. There are too many vegetables in it to make that safe.

A recipe is always canned, as you indicated, by the ingredient that requires the highest pressure or pressure canning, versus water bath canning.

Oops — waterless canning

Read your stuff all the time. I just did a really stupid thing and need your advice.

I am pressure canning some beef, and it's far from my first time. It was while I was unloading the first 14 pints that I realized that I never put water in the canner. The jars have all sealed, the canner stayed in one piece, but I'm wondering if the meat will be okay. What do you think?

Mary Wolfe, Pennsylvania

Wow! That's a new one on me! Here's my guess: probably, your meat is okay, as the jars have all sealed and there probably was some steam generated by moisture in the jars during processing. But I'd mark the jars and be awful sure I checked each one carefully upon use. Look at the meat, open a jar, making sure it is still sealed well, then smell the meat. If all is okay, be sure to bring the meat to boiling temperature for 15 minutes before eating.

I'll bet you never do that again. How scary! I have visions of a warped canner and blowing up jars!

Running the pressure canner without water

I'm a regular cover-to-cover reader of BHM, *and I really appreciate your section on food preparation. However, I must take exception to the answer you gave to Mary Wolfe in Issue #126, Nov/Dec 2010 issue (Oops — Waterless Canning). She forgot to put water into her canner before pressure-processing pint-jars of beef, but the jar lids did seal properly. Your reply:*

"... Here's my guess: probably your meat is okay, as the jars all sealed and there probably was some steam generated by moisture in the jars during processing. But I'd mark the jars and be awful sure I checked each one carefully upon use. Look at the meat, open a jar, making sure it is still sealed well, then smell the meat. If all is okay, be sure to bring the meat to boiling temperature for 15 minutes before eating ..."

*My comments are based on 20 years' experience as a Food Safety Inspector, including numerous cannery inspections, completing the standard "Better Process Control" classes several times (*highly recommended for* *home canners, and required by law for canning retort. Operators — see your state college food science departments), and completion of an Advanced Canning course provided by the FDA. (I'm now retired.) While I'm not a full-fledged Food Science Professor, or a certified "Process Authority" for a cannery, my professional opinion is as follows:*

1. The jars of processed meat have well-sealed lids: This means that the contents of the container reached at least boiling temperature (212°F), producing steam and forming a vacuum when cooling. However, there is no way to know whether the contents reached the required full-processing pressure and temperature (10-15 psi of pressure/240°F-250°F temperature), and for how long. The boiling temperature most likely killed all the food-poisoning and spoilage bacteria, but not the most critical spores of the botulinum bacteria.

2. Well-sealed lids also show that there was no re-contamination after processing. But what is still present and viable, like the spores, can still be a problem.

3. The time and pressure/temperature specifications in our canning manuals depend on heat transfer by the steam in the pressure cooker-canning vessel, continuously and to the entire surface of the jar and lid for proper heat penetration to the coldest spot inside the jar/container. Without water in the canner, a) heat was probably only transferred through the bottoms of the jars; b) the jars were probably insulated somewhat by air remaining inside the canner, and c) it is highly unlikely that the proper temperature/pressure could be maintained through the cook.

Conclusion: It is highly likely that botulinum spores were still viable in these containers of meat, and produced botulism toxin in these jars within a week or two.

Regarding your recommended handling procedures:

1. Check for sealed lids: Yes, this shows that at least a boiling temperature was achieved inside the jar, and there was no re-contamination after processing. (But botulism is still possible.)

2. Checking appearance and smell of the product upon opening: Yes, this shows that (more easily killed) spoilage bacteria were destroyed. But, Botulinum spores, bacteria, and toxin is odorless and does not produce visible changes. Also, do not taste, even a little bit, to go along with your smell check. Botulism toxin is the most deadly poison known — even a fingertip dipped in the food for a taste can kill.

3. Bring the meat to a boiling temperature for 15 minutes before eating. Yes. This procedure will destroy any harmful bacteria, as well as botulism toxin, that is in the food. (However, please be careful how you handle the utensils. For example, if a spoon is used to empty the jar into a pan for cooking, the spoon's surface may be contaminated and transfer residue elsewhere.) This cooking procedure has probably saved hundreds of lives over the years.

As an alternative procedure, may I also suggest that it is safe to take the marked jars and run them through another canning cook process, without opening them? Just follow the same time and pressure temperature recommendations for the original food product. This may "mush" fragile vegetables like asparagus, but meats will only soften a bit more in texture. There would be no safety issues with storing them away again.

Again, Jackie, I greatly appreciate your column, and this is the first thing I've ever had any concerns about. Keep up the good work!

Peter Regan, Oregon

Peter, you are right. The steam generated from the meat broth may not have been enough to have safely processed the meat. I guess the old adage is right; when in doubt … reprocess.

84 year-old auntie never used pressure canner

My aunt (the matriarch of our family) is 84 years old, and my garden this year has been fantastic! I asked my aunt for canning advice (Dad, her brother, was the cook and he's been gone for 20 years). She is telling me that she never had a pressure cooker and always used a hot water bath canner (the one I have is her sister's). She is telling me how she does string beans, peppers, squash, and corn (and other fruits and vegetables). Most of these are recommended in the "Ball Blue Book" to be pressure cooked … but how can I argue with almost 84 years of experience? Especially since I've been eating these preserves for 44 years?

Robert Stalker, New York

Yes, yes, I know of many "aunts" just like yours. And yes, they did can for years using only a water bath canner. But yes, you can die from eating Auntie's water bath processed vegetables!

Did you get that? The dangerous bacteria that can kill you are *not* all that common, but they are around, in the soil, in the air, maybe on Auntie's hands even. All it takes is one batch of those vegetables, canned unsafely in a water bath canner, and you are very sick or DEAD. Personally, I don't want to risk it when pressure canning is *so* easy and *so* safe.

Buy a big enough canner

I am purchasing a pressure canner for my son for a birthday present at his request. He said I should write to you and ask that you recommend a few brands. I did see a Presto on the net but did not wish to get it if it is not going to last. Price was about $90. Can you give me some help?

Debbie

Presto is a good brand of canner. Many are in use that are more than 50 years old. Personally, I prefer a gasketless canner so that you do not have to change gaskets through the years. Unfortunately, these canners cost a little more to purchase. I believe Mirro makes a line of these canners. It really doesn't matter which brand you choose, but be sure you get a large enough canner. Some folks have been fooled into buying a small "pressure cooker/canner," which doesn't even hold quart jars and makes home canning a nightmare. Get your son a larger canner that will hold at least five quart jars and he will be eternally grateful.

Minomatic canner

I recently bought an old Minomatic "jiggly weight" canner at a thrift store. It didn't include the manual, but for $12 who's complaining? I've already canned veggie soup and spaghetti sauce with it and I think it went okay. (I've eaten the results and am still alive!) I followed the general rules for pressure canning in the "Ball Blue Book," but a *few things were kind of unclear. How long should it take for the weight to jiggle when I put it on? I exhausted the air for 10 minutes before putting it on but after I put it on it took almost 10 minutes more to start going! There was some questionable hissing and sputtering coming from the right side and under the weight around the valve. The side stopped letting off steam when the weight started to go. Does this mean it has sealed? I started timing then. Is it supposed to take so long to seal? Lastly, how will I know when the seal needs to be replaced? Any advice would be greatly appreciated!*

Confused Canner, New York

There is no set time on how long it takes the weight to jiggle after you exhaust the air and put it in place. The same holds true with gauge type canners. It depends on how many jars of what type of food is in them. Don't try to hurry things or begin timing too soon. That is how people get into trouble by not processing the food long enough.

There is usually some miscellaneous hissing before things get under way. As long as it stops, you are probably alright.

The gasket needs to be replaced if it feels stiff, sort of hard, and/or steam escapes excessively and the jiggler weight doesn't jiggle or jiggles weakly.

Small vs. big canner

I have a 21 quart Presto canner with a pressure gauge that I have been using for 40 years, and it is still giving good service. I have just bought for $20 a second-hand 22-quart Mirro canner that uses weights. I haven't picked it up yet.

Many times I have just 2-4 pints of food I would like to can, but I do not want to get out my big canner. Do you know of a small canner (not one that holds seven quart or nine pint jars) that would be suitable for just a few jars? Where could I purchase this canning equipment by mail? Is there any real advantage energy-wise and time-wise to using a small canner over using what I already have?

I just finished reading your piece on canning meat. Have you ever canned fish? Around here, when the carp are running, if they are well prepared for processing, they make the most wonderful canned "salmon." Beats any fish I have ever bought in the store, and carp are considered junk fish.

Jean Dittmer, Missouri

I understand your problem, but I've found that it's just as easy to use the big canner for even those odd small batches that we come up with during the harvest season. The only small canners available are the so-called canner/pressure cooker combination that are not recommended for canning even small batches.

Yes, I've canned fish. I haven't canned carp because they don't live where we do. But I have canned sucker, smoked and fresh, and mountain whitefish with great results, as well as salmon, trout, steelhead, panfish, and northern pike. With today's game laws, we have to be *very* careful not to "possess" too many fish in our pantry. It used to be that the term "possess" meant how many fish you had on your person one day. We fished a lot and stocked up the pantry because we never ate all of our legal limit for a day. Now you can get into *big* trouble doing that in most states. Just be aware and check your fish and game laws.

Using a pressure cooker as a pressure canner

Can you use a pressure "cooker" as a pressure "canner?"

Roy Sherman, California

I'm sure some folks get by doing this, but I would not advise it. First of all, the pressure cooker does not have a rack to keep the jars off the bottom of the pot, as does a pressure canner. Second, the cooker is much too small for any serious canning. And finally, the pressure cooker is built for cooking in mind, not canning, and I have doubts as to whether it would hold exact pressures for the length of time necessary for processing home canned foods safely.

High altitude canning

I grow a lot of tomatoes in my garden each year but, as I live at 2500 feet above sea level, I am afraid to can them. I bought a pressure canner, but am afraid to use it due to all the warnings about acidic foods canned at altitude. Can you tell me a safe way to can tomatoes at my home and is there a chemical test (think litmus) to see if already canned food is safe to eat, i.e. without botulism?

Elizabeth MacLeod, California

You don't have to pressure can tomatoes. A simple water bath canner is plenty good and safe too. If you don't have a water bath canner, you can just use your pressure canner without shutting the lid and putting on the weight or shutting the petcock. I canned tons of tomatoes at altitudes from 6,000 feet in New Mexico to 7,400 feet in Montana with absolutely no problems.

Your canned tomatoes are perfectly good to eat if you followed directions and the jars are sealed. If they look fine and smell fine, they will be fine. As you gain experience, you'll soon laugh at your old fears and begin to get excited about home canning as so many others have.

Canning on the verge of high altitude

We will be building a house on the top of the ridge that runs across our property. We're planning on taking up canning as we get our gardens up and running. The top of the ridge is at 1,003 feet elevation. If I set up canning in the basement it will be below 1,000 feet. In the first floor kitchen it will be above 1,000 feet. With it being right on the line, do I need to use the higher pressure when canning?

Jason M. Waldo, Tennessee

I, personally, wouldn't worry a bit about canning at a higher pressure because you are right on the line of 1,000 feet. In the old days, the increase began at 2,000 feet. A foot or two won't make a difference. Enjoy your new homestead!

A problem using gasketless canner

For years I wanted a pressure canner. I researched on the web and felt that I wanted the top of the line All-American gasketless canner. My husband bought one for my birthday in March. I had never pressure canned; however, I had watched a friend do it. My first and only attempt was with spinach from my garden. I had water bath canned for years so filling the jars was no problem. When I tried to bring the canner up to pressure there seemed to be a lot of steam escaping from the "seal." There are both a dial gauge and weight. I was never sure when the steam had "exhausted" enough. It seemed to take forever and I was afraid the canner would boil dry. As we are at 3,000 feet, I used the weight on 15 lbs. The dial never read higher than 12 pounds and I was never sure how much the weight should rock back and forth. I was really disappointed and seven months later I am afraid to eat the spinach or do any more canning. I really want to be successful but no one I know has a gasketless canner. I'm beginning to wish I had bought a cheaper one with a gasket. Can you help me?

Theresa Bailey, Idaho

This is not normal. Either there is a defect in the canner (unlikely) or you didn't have the lid down tight enough to the body of the canner. With your canner, you received a warranty card and instruction booklet with a consumer helpline number. Don't be shy about calling the company. They want you to be happy with your new canner and can help you solve your problem. If your canner didn't have a number or at least an address to contact, go back to your store and ask for one. There *is* help.

I have used a gasketless canner for more than 30 years now and have had absolutely no problem with it. Any new endeavor is a bit frightening, but keep at it and you'll succeed.

You can also take your canner to your home extension office (usually located in the courthouse) and have them help you get started. I would call ahead to make sure someone knowledgeable is there when you arrive. This service is also free.

Canning on a woodstove

I am interested in canning venison and salmon with a large pressure canner, but I'd like to do it on a small cabin woodstove. I have read several good books on canning from the BHM *bookstore, but there's no mention of the heat source other than it must remain steady. What say you on this matter, Jackie?*

Thomas Brower, Oregon

I've canned on everything from a rock fire ring with a grate on it (difficult with a pressure canner, but easy with a water bath), to a camp stove (not so bad with either), a wood kitchen range and, of course, a regular gas range. The one problem I noticed when canning on a Coleman type camp stove is that the canner with the jars in it weighs so much, the stove kind of gets tippy unless you have it on a solid table. Instead of the lightweight Coleman stove, I switched to the cheap two or three-burner gas stoves you can buy through most cheaper tool catalogs, such as Northern Tool. They cost about the same as the Coleman stoves, but stay much steadier while canning. Good canning!

Water seeping into canning jars

I am trying to can shrimp pickle. The main concern is that there should be no water content in the bottle. But when I put it in the pressure cooker water leaked into the bottles. I pressure cooked for about 20 minutes. I do not have a very big pressure cooker. It holds only three pint size bottles. Please let me know what mistake I am making.

Ratna

Sorry you are having such trouble. My first suggestion is to go out and buy a larger pressure canner. The so-called "pressure cooker/canners" just don't do a good job of canning. A new moderately-sized pressure canner will cost about $110. But if you can't afford that, you can usually pick up a good used one at a yard sale, estate sale, flea market, or thrift store for less than $25. One of mine cost just $5, and came with the instruction manual and all equipment such as jar lifter and funnel.

Are you using canning jars? Some folks get into trouble like yours by using bottles which previously held such things as tartar sauce or horseradish. These do not take a two-piece canning lid and are not adequate for home canning.

Finally, make sure you have followed the basic pressure canning steps. These may vary a little bit, but are pretty standard. Always check your recipe for exact directions and make sure your recipe came from a canning book, manual, or other reliable source.

The basic pressure canning steps are:

1. Place food in clean canning jar, leaving the required headroom (empty space at the top of the jar). This is typically one inch.

2. Wipe the rim of the jar clean with a damp cloth.

3. Place a hot, previously boiled lid on the jar and screw down the ring firmly tight.

4. Place the jars on rack in a canner which has about one inch of water in it to create steam. This may vary with your own canner, but there should never be excessive water in the canner. Lock the lid on tightly.

5. Turn on the heat with the petcock(s) open.

6. Exhaust steam forcefully for several minutes. Again, check your own canner's directions.

7. Close the petcock(s) and allow pressure to build to that needed to process the food (typically 10 pounds unless you live at an altitude higher than 1,000 feet, then check your canning book).

8. Hold the pressure at this reading for the entire time you must process the food.

9. When this time is up, turn off the heat and wait for the pressure to drop to zero.

10. Carefully open the petcock(s) and allow any steam to escape.

11. Open the canner and remove the jars to a dry folded towel in a draft free area to cool. Do not touch the jars until they are cool.

12. Check for complete seal by feeling with one finger for a tight indentation in the center of each lid. There should be absolutely no give.

I've been canning all my life and have never had water seep into a jar. So I'm confident that if you give these hints a try, you'll soon be smiling over your newly canned food.

Greasy liquid in canner is from pressure difference

In reading your column in the July/August issue (Issue #112), I noticed a question on page 72 titled "Greasy liquid in canner." I, too, had a similar problem when I first started canning with a pressure canner. That was years ago. I had taken a course on steam boilers so I realized what the problem was. It's especially noticed when canning beets; the water in the pressure canner will turn red from the beet juice. The grease, or beet juice, whatever,

*that's in the jars (it only happens with jars, not cans) tends
to force its way out from under the sealing lid and out of
the jars if too much differential pressure exists between the
interior of the jar and the surrounding pressure canner.
This is why it is important to keep an eye on the pressure
and not let it swing up and down. It requires a bit of at-
tention to be sure. But I've found the main reason for the
contents of the jars to end up in the water of the pressure
canner is the cooling off of the pressure too quickly. So
many instructions tell a person to do this, or not to do that,
but they, so it would seem to me, don't explain why! If the
pressure canner is cooled too quickly, (opening a petcock
or relief valve causes this cooling in the extreme) it causes
a pressure differential between the inside and the outside
of the jars, the greater pressure being within the jars. This
causes the contents inside the jar to want to force their way
out of the jar from under the lid and into the surrounding
water. You then get the "greasy liquid in the canner," or
the very red water when canning beets. Of course whatever
comes out is lost from the jar contents itself. The solution
is to cool down the pressure canner very slowly. I usually
cover mine with hot mitts and towels. Because it takes a
while for the pressure canner to cool to zero pressure when
covered, I invested in a second one.*

*I recently canned some smoked ham hocks. Of course I
had to cook and de-bone them first. I found by cooking
them at 15 pounds pressure, then relieving the pressure
quickly (I opened the petcock), that the meat was (blown?)
off the bones; at least it came off much easier than any
other way.*

Bert Maupin, Alaska

I agree with you, Bert, that a lot of times the pressure fluctuations or someone "tweaking" the pressure petcock to hurry things up, back to zero, causes liquid to blow out of the jars. Don't, however, slow things down too much. I waited too long once, after my canner had reached zero — several hours, in fact (I fell asleep!), and every one of those jars of corn had a failed seal after a week in the pantry.

I always just turn off my heat and let things cool off a little at a time, then as soon as it's reached zero, I exhaust any remaining dribbles of steam and take off the lid. By doing this, I very seldom have much "goop" blown out of my jars.

Using vinegar in a canner

In regards to using vinegar in the water of a pressure canner to keep the jars clean (Issue #103), vinegar does work well in the water. However, if your canner is aluminum, it will pit the metal if left to stand any length of time. I found this out the hard way. Now I use rainwater when available, or even melt some snow down. Distilled water works well but isn't free.

I started rinsing out my canner with baking soda water after using the vinegar method, and this also seems to have stopped any further damage.

Cheryl Olson, Wisconsin

Great idea, Cheryl. I just don't worry about having a coating on my jars, as I always wash them off in hot soapy water before I put them on my pantry shelves anyway. I'm also a lazy canner.

Canning on an electric stove

I've been canning for years, usually with a boiling water bath canner, occasionally with a pressure canner. Lately, because of the shape our country is in and because of your catching enthusiasm for canning, I have been doing a lot of pressure canning. My canner is about 6 years old but hasn't been used much until recently. It is a weighted gauge type and looks like new. My problem is that I cook on an electric stove. We don't have natural gas where I live in Maine. We can't afford a new gas stove with the propane hookup, so I am stuck with electricity. It is VERY difficult to keep steady pressure with an electric stove. While I rarely let the pressure drop below 10 pounds, it often fluctuates from 10 pounds to higher, and then back down to 10 again, no matter now careful I am. Because of this, I often lose liquid from my jars, and a lot of that liquid is grease, since I'm canning many meat dishes. The jars all seal fine. But I worry about their contents. I've been told as long as they're sealed, the contents are fine even if they are unattractive. I wonder though if the seals will last. I just canned 16 jars of barbecued ribs and I'd hate to lose them six months down the line. Do you have problems with jars losing liquids? Do you obtain a seal if they do, and how long does your seal last?

Melanie

I sympathize with your problems regulating your electric stove for canning. When I first started canning, it was on an electric stove, and I too had trouble. I solved it by switching to using my wood burning kitchen range. But for you, perhaps an easier fix would be to buy a two-burner propane stove. These are available at most discount tool catalogs, such as Harbor Freight and Northern Tool, or your local propane dealer. They cost about $40-100. (They are used for "camping" and are not a typical kitchen stove, only a basic countertop, two burner unit.) Then you will just need a 40-pound or even a 100-pound propane tank with a hose and regulator and you are in business. Many propane companies simply sell you the propane and furnish the bottle at no cost. The hose and regulator are very inexpensive.

With this setup you can home can, regulating the heat with precision. Voilà, no more boiled out liquids! And you can cook if there's a power outage, as well.

Yes, I've had liquids boiled partially out of jars I've canned. Usually when I get interrupted by something while I can and the pressure rises, then falls, as I discover the problem. It is unattractive, but I've never had any problem with the seals failing. As with all home canned food, always examine each jar before opening it to be sure the seal is tight; look at the food and smell it after opening it. Just to be sure.

Water bath canning

Don't use a water bath to can green beans

I am in dire need of a good recipe for canning green beans using the hot bath method. Someone has given me green beans and I really need a good recipe.

Maxine Reed, Tennessee

Sorry, Maxine, you cannot safely can beans in a hot water bath canner unless they are pickled. Beans are low acid, as are all vegetables, meat, and fish. Because they are a low-acid food, this means that under certain conditions, dangerous bacteria such as *Clostridium botulinum* could be canned right along with your beans. This bacteria grows everywhere, from your soil to your countertops.

The spores, which are the dormant form of this bacteria, are not deadly, but when they are canned with your water bathed beans they are not killed and can live to produce a very deadly toxin that is not killed at 212 degrees, which is the temperature of your boiling water bath. They are killed when they are subjected to the 240 degrees in your pressure canner (10 pounds pressure).

Now, I know, and have been told countless times, that folks used to water bath their green beans, and still do. This is true. But it's too dangerous to do, and I simply won't do it, nor will I advise anyone to do it either. People can go years eating water bathed beans and other low-acid foods, and then suddenly hit a jar that is toxic. It's like playing Russian roulette. I won't play; and I hope you won't either.

Dangers of water bath canning

I am trying to find my mom a recipe for water bath canning for green beans.

She's looking for just a basic recipe that uses some type of acid, lemon juice, etc.

She canned like this years ago but has forgotten how.

She does not own a pressure cooker and has no intentions of buying one.

Vera

Sorry Vera, but there's just no safe recipe for water bath canning green beans unless she pickles them. For instance she could make dilly beans, mustard yellow bean pickles, etc. Many, many people used to water bath process their beans, corn, and even meat. But it just is not safe. One of the biggest dangers is botulism, a sure killer that is both odorless and tasteless. Using a water bath to can low-acid items like green beans is the same as letting your children play with a loaded gun.

I'm sorry your mom is not interested in buying a pressure canner. They are so easy and safe to use. And the canning takes much less time, too.

Canning low-acid foods with the utmost safety

In the January/February 2002 issue of BHM, *you gave advice to Mary Stoneberg on home canning. "You cannot safely use a water bath canner for green beans." I beg to differ.*

I will be 65 years old in October. My mother, who is 90, and the entire family home canned in the '40s and '50s and myself in the '60s all using hot bath canners of some type. With a family of eight, the entire family worked like Trojans to can produce to carry us through the next year. We used a #3 wash tub, a discarded copper kettle that was formerly a whiskey still, and a cast iron wash pot to boil our filled jars in for three to four hours using any scrap wood we had to keep the fire going for this long period of time. This may not be the conventional way to preserve food but some of us could not afford a pressure canner thus we made do with what we had. We canned snap beans, crowder peas, butter beans, pears, huckleberries, etc. and probably had a thousand jars of quart canned produce in the wash house storage for winter, all by using the hot water bath boiling system.

Needless to say, we eight are all still living.

Maxine Ramsay, Mississippi

You'll notice in my answer to Mary, I did not say you could not can green beans in a water bath canner. I said you could not *safely* can green beans or any other low-acid food in a boiling water bath canner. There is a great difference.

Yes, I know that thousands of folks, including some of my ancestors, canned low-acid foods, including vegetables and even meat, using a boiling water bath canner. Back in Minnesota, several of my older neighbor ladies still do their vegetables that way. But it just is not safe.

No matter how long you boil that water bath canner full of jars, the temperature never gets high enough to kill the toxin-producing spores of *Clostridium botulinum*, the bacteria that produces deadly food poisoning.

Clostridium botulinum is not a common bacteria around home food, so in most cases you can get away with canning those green beans in a water bath canner by boiling for three to four hours. But if you are unlucky, you may feed your child deadly poison by accident. Personally, I don't want to risk it. It's sort of like playing Russian roulette with a machine gun. Probably you will get away with putting that gun to your head and pulling the trigger dozens of times. But it only takes one bullet to end the game.

I know that in the past, folks just couldn't afford a pressure canner in many cases. But that's not the case today. I've bought used pressure canners in working condition for $5 and $10. That's a good price to pay for *safe* home canning.

Canning mistake?

I have just started canning and I think I made a mistake and I am wondering how crucial a mistake it is. I made pickles on the weekend and I water bathed them but I did not cover the jars with water (I got confused and thought that I should keep water from going over the tops). I sterilized the jars and lids before filling them, the brine boiled up nice and hot and all of my jars sealed perfectly. Is this a terrible problem? I don't want to poison my family.

Deana Lehmann Mooers

It's probably just fine. Certainly not a terrible problem. And you will not poison your family with your pickles.

The absolute worst thing that could happen is that the seals could fail. Unnoticed, any pickles that are not in the vinegar might turn dark or go soft. But pickles are so acidic that some recipes for pickles do not even require water bath processing. The reason that the water should go over the jars is so you ensure that all of the food and the complete jar is equally heated. Just look at your pickles before serving them. If they look good, smell good, and are not gooshy soft, they will make you proud.

Steam canning

I love using my water bath canner for tomatoes and fruits, but I've seen steam canners for sale in catalogs. The ads claim they save on water, which is especially interesting to me, a municipal water user who's charged per usage. In your opinion, are these canners just as good as a water bath canner?

Kristin Radtke, Wisconsin

No. These steam canners are not recommended for canning (no matter what the ads say), as it is not certain how much heat actually reaches the centers of the food in the center of the jars. You can save money and water when using a water bath canner by reusing the water for several batches of jars — unless one breaks, of course. Just add enough to bring the level up to two inches over the tops of the jars. You don't need to dump the whole thing every time. I also use my "used" canning water to water my indoor fruit trees and other large plants.

Stock pot as a water bath canner

About the pressure cooker, is that needed or can you just put a rack in a big stock pot and follow the instructions? Like I said I've never done this before and apologize if my questions sound rather idiotic.

Stephanie Payne

You can use a stock pot or any other large container as a hot water bath canner. My grandmother used to use her copper boiler to can peaches and other fruits in. You do need to keep the jars off the bottom of the container or they will break. A wire rack works great. You have to have a big enough container or pot to allow the water to maintain a rolling boil an inch or more over the jars, and a top is necessary to quickly bring the water to a rolling boil and keep it there for processing.

All low-acid foods, such as vegetables, meat and poultry, and any mixes (soups, stews, etc.), must be pressure canned using a pressure canner, not a pressure cooker, which is not large enough, nor intended for canning.

Vinegar in canning water

When I use a water bath canner, I add about ¼ cup of white vinegar to the water in which the jars are placed. The vinegar prevents minerals in the water from discoloring the jars during the boiling process.

Bruce Clark, New York

Good idea, Bruce. I never thought of that although I use vinegar to boil out my tea kettle when it gets mineral deposits in it. It'd save time washing the film off the jars, for sure.

Lids and jars

Small-batch canning

I have a pretty large canner and would like to can only maybe 3 or 4 pints at a time. Sometimes I have leftovers that I would like to can for later use. Are there any problems with doing this? Maybe the jars getting broken, etc.? I would like to buy a small cooker/canner (about 8 quarts) but just don't have the money.

Shirley Owens, Florida

There is no minimum amount of jars needed to fill a canner; you can process one pint, if you need to, but it's wasting fuel and time to do so in most cases. With three or four pints, it becomes much more economical. You'd be surprised at how quickly those 3-4 pint batches add up! Do remember to process your leftovers at the longest time required for any one ingredient — usually meat. And remember, too, that some vegetables, rice, and noodles get mushy when cooked fully, then canned. They're still edible, just mushy.

Sterilizing jars

What is the proper way to sterilize jars? After washing in soapy water, my grandmother just rinsed them in bleach water. I boil the water, but that's such a hassle. My friend says just run the jars in the dishwasher. Once they've been sterilized, how long can they sit before they are no longer sterile? After boiling them, I turn them upside down in the dish drainer and cover with a flour-sack towel. I usually need to add more water to the canner and bring it to a boil for processing. It may take me another 15-30 minutes before I have all the jars filled and ready to go into the canner. (Okay, I'm very slow!) Anyway, I've always wondered if I should do as my grandmother did and just leave the jars in the hot bleach water until I was ready to use them. I don't have a dishwasher, but it would give me one more reason to get one if that would get the jars sterile.

Charlene Nelson, North Dakota

To sterilize canning jars, simmer them in a boiling water bath canner for 10 minutes. Then keep them in that hot water until you are ready to use them. Take them out of the water, one jar at a time, turn upside down briefly to drain the water out, then right side up for a few seconds while you prepare to fill them. The heat will adequately dry the jar. This is simple and also keeps the jars hot, preventing any cracks while you fill them with hot foods. (A cool jar filled with a hot food will sometimes crack.)

Fill the jars, then place the filled jars on a folded dry towel until all are filled. Then refill your canner, if necessary, and bring it up to very hot again, and put the jars in. There! You're ready to go, with sterile, filled jars.

Boil the canning lids?

In all of Jackie's recipes for canning, she tells folks to boil the lids. On the box the lids come in it specifically says "do not boil."

Carolyn Lucas, Michigan

I don't know what kind of jar lids you use, but I've read three different new boxes of mine, and all say "simmer, then keep in warm water until use." My canning manuals all say to do this, as well, except this year's *Ball Blue Book*. It says "simmer" but do not boil. It seems that folks were letting their lids boil dry, then the seal compound on the lids failed. So "simmer" your lids at 180 degrees, then keep in the hot water, or pour boiling water over them and keep them in hot water. I will refrain from using "boiling" in the future.

Canning jars

Thank you so much for all of your information on canning over the years. Your article has been helpful.

Whenever I find canning jars at yard sales, I look for Ball/Kerr with no chips or cracks. Recently my husband's grandma gave us five boxes of glass jars. While many of them are "recent," there are some that look like quart canning jars, but I am leery. Some actually have Ball printed very small on the bottom, while others have a number stamped on them. The threads look like they are canning jars, too. My mother-in-law thought there was a universal number you could go by, but wasn't sure. They look pressure canning grade, but I won't chance it unless I know for sure. Please note there were obvious jars that were mayo, pickles, and commercial jelly jars. Thank you for any info you can give.

Trina McMillen, Oregon

I'm not as fussy about my canning jars as some folks are. I can in any sound jar that will accept a standard canning lid and ring, allowing it to be screwed down firmly tight. And I include mayonnaise jars, too. I've successfully canned foods requiring pressure canning like meat, corn, and beans in these jars and have had no more breakage than when I used big-name jars. One thing I have done to make sure I have less breakage is to always warm up the canner before I place hot jars into them. In the past, I didn't do this and found that I frequently had a jar or two break out the bottom from the old cold-hot conflict. Since I began doing this, I have had very few jars break.

Sounds like you made quite a haul. Good for you.

For community canning, try the local LDS church

Where can a person buy metal cans to can in? Where could a person get information on starting a community canning place?

Pete Zahradnicek, South Dakota

You can buy metal cans and sealers for them at Aaoob Foods (www.aaoobfoods.com). You can also call your local Latter Day Saints church and ask them who you might talk to regarding a community canning kitchen. Many LDS churches have their own community canning kitchens that they will share with others.

Canning in gallon jars

What is the possibility of canning in one-gallon jars? I have many. I see products are canned in one-gallon cans in the food stores.

I have also been looking for information about how to use a pressure canner on a wood stove.

David Dawson, Texas

Sorry, David, but you can't can in one-gallon jars. First off, you can't find canning lids and rings that will fit them. Then, the experts advise us against canning in even half-gallon jars now, for fear that we won't get the food hot enough in the center of these larger jars for safe process-ing. I still use half-gallon jars, but only for soups, fruits, and juices.

It is certainly possible to use a pressure canner on a wood stove. I canned on a wood stove alone, for years and years; I had no "back-up" stove. When you get to know your stove and wood well, it is fairly easy to learn just how hot a fire you'll need to maintain during your processing. Instead of turning your burner heat up or down to regulate your heat, you gently drag your canner over the firebox to "turn up" the heat or away from the firebox to "turn down" the heat. It *is* easier to can on a wood stove, using a canner with a weight instead of a dial, as the weight jiggles and self-ad-justs quite a bit, allowing more leeway so you don't have to slide the canner so much. My big canner has a dial gauge, so I learned to keep a good fire and position my canner so I didn't need to move it as much; it does take some practice.

One thing to consider, especially when buying a wood range that you'll be canning on, is making sure that there is room for your canner between your cook top and the warming oven or shelf. One stove that I bought didn't have enough room for my big canner, like my old stove did, so I had to buy a smaller, used canner. I didn't plan on *that*!

Canning in half-gallon jars

Is it okay to can food in half-gallon jars?

Several readers

I have canned in half-gallon jars for years, but now experts do not recommend it. Personally, I have no problem with canning liquid-based foods such as juices or broth in them, as you are *sure* that the correct temperatures necessary for safe processing are reached in the *center* of the jars. The danger lies in densely packed jars of such foods as meats (roasts, steaks, etc.), corn, baked beans, etc. With these foods in a larger jar, you are never sure that the required temperature for safe processing reaches the center of the jar, or if it does, does it remain at this temperature for the entire time required for safe processing? Better safe than sorry; don't use the half-gallon jars for *any* type of dense foods. Safer yet, only use them for fruit juices and storing dry foods on your pantry shelves.

Quarts or pints

I am a new subscriber to Backwoods Home Magazine *and am enjoying your articles very much. I recently purchased the "Emergency Preparedness and Survival Guide." In the book you have a list of 1 year's food supply based on your family of three. I am curious as to why*

most of your home canned items are in pint jars? Don't
they take up more pantry space than quart jars would? I
must admit that I have more quart jars than pints. I have
just finished reading your article in Issue #114, (Nov/Dec
2008) and your recipes sound yummy.
Carmen Hitchcock, Colorado

I used to can nearly exclusively in quarts. But I've found
that three people use pints more than quarts, especially
when you are making mixed recipes; you don't always use
a quart of carrots, corn, peas, or whatever. I have a small
refrigerator and do not like "old" leftovers, and in an emergency situation, there is often no refrigeration. So I use the
pints and even half-pints now. It makes the food I can go
further and some things, like meat, are often just used as
a flavoring in a recipe. For instance, I often scramble up
a pan of eggs and toss in a half-pint of diced ham. With a
jar that size there are no leftovers. I hate waste, and cringe
whenever a leftover goes to the dogs or chickens. My pantry shelves are close together and very deep. Yes, quarts
would fill up the shelves with food. But for me, pints and
half-pints fill them with more usable food. But, of course,
I still can a whole lot of food in quarts. I have hundreds of
quart jars full in my pantry right now. I save them for things
like turkey breast, roast venison, ham slices, chicken and
noodles, baked beans, stews, soups, spaghetti sauce, chili,
etc. that are nearly meals in themselves.

Smaller jars

Probably a silly question, but a few years ago I canned
some pickled red cabbage and some corn relish in half-
pint jars. Since I am the only one who likes these items,

63

sometimes I would have to toss the remainder of the jar if I didn't get it used up quickly enough. I have some smaller than half-pint jars. Would there be any problem with using these smaller jars in the hot water bath?

Ruth Dixon, Oregon

Absolutely not. I do the same thing myself. I also can up these small jars full of chicken, pork, venison, and beef pieces to add to casseroles, etc. for flavoring. It sure makes a little canned meat go a long, long way! And with the future meat prices, hold on to your hat!

Wire bail canning jars

I recently got a cache of about 20 dozen old wire bail canning jars for free. Every book on canning tells me to buy new rubbers every year. Is this necessary?

I believe my grandmother reused rubbers that were in very good condition. I don't plan on using any that came with the jars because of the age.

Kenneth J. Pearl Sr., Massachusetts

Yes, you pretty much have to use new rubbers each year as the rubbers get hard after the jars have been sealed for a while. And hard rubbers will not seal properly. Be sure you only use the glass top jars for low-acid foods, such as fruits and pickles, because there is no way to tell if the jars have sealed or not, as you can with modern two-piece lids which indent in the center when sealed. You wouldn't want to chance eating foods that might be spoiled.

Canning in tin cans

I was wondering; I have done canning before and am doing it now again. I purchased some tin cans and the machine that goes with them. I have never done this before. Have never seen tin cans for canning, but it is in an old time book I have. Just wondered if you knew of anyone that has used them before?

Judy

The only book that I've seen that has instructions for canning in tin cans is the older *Putting Foods By* by Ruth Hertzberg, Beatrice Vaughan, and Janet Greene. Many folks have put home canned foods up in tin cans. One problem with canning foods at home with tin cans is that other than bulging cans and spoiled food later during storage, there's no real way to know if the cans have indeed sealed properly. When home canning with the common, two-piece lids you can actually see the lid sucked tightly in when the seal is good, making this a safer method of canning at home. And then there is the cost of buying new cans for every batch of canning that you plan on doing. Canning jars and the rings are reusable; you only need to buy inexpensive new lids each year.

One hint in canning with tin cans is to "sacrifice" a couple of cans before you actually can. Partially fill them with water, seal the can with your sealer, then drop them into a kettle of boiling water. If there are air bubbles coming from around the sealed rim, your seal is not good and your can sealer must be adjusted again.

Be sure you use instructions meant for tin cans, as the canning process is definitely different than when you home can with glass jars.

Procedure for canning in tin cans

Can you please tell me the procedure for canning in tin cans? I have the sealer and cans, and I have made a few test cans, but I am unsure how to actually pressure cook the contents, then seal the lids.

Matt, Wisconsin

I'll be glad to. I don't use tin cans because of the cost of the non-reusable cans. Jars can be used, year after year, generation after generation. But, seeing how you have the cans and the sealer, here's how to do it.

First, be absolutely sure your sealer is working properly, creating air-tight seals on your cans. You can do this by filling a can half full of water, then dropping it into a kettle full of boiling water. Watch for air bubbles escaping from the can. If there are none, your sealer is fine. If there are, adjust your sealer to crimp tighter.

All food processed in tin cans must be heated to 170°F before sealing the can, in order to drive out any air in the food, as this air cannot escape as it does when you use jars with two-piece lids. You can do this by filling the cans, then placing them in a water bath canner rack, with water to within two inches of the top of the cans. Put the lid on the canner and boil until the internal temperature of the food in the cans reaches 170°F. Wipe the can rim, then immediately seal with a lid and proceed to the next step called for, either water bath canning or pressure canning.

The next difference between canning with cans and canning with jars is that when you remove the tin cans from the canner following processing, you must cool them quickly by immersing them in a sink full of cold water. (If you did this with jars, they would shatter.)

Just like canning with jars, each high-acid food, such as fruit, is canned using a water bath canner, with differing lengths of time for processing. And low-acid foods such as vegetables and meats are canned using a pressure canner, also for various lengths of time, depending on what you are canning. The only book I have seen which addresses using tin cans in home canning is *Putting Food By* by Ruth Hertzberg, Beatrice Vaughan, and Janet Green (Stephen Green Press). You may want to pick up a copy so you will have the times needed for each food you wish to can.

Using old lids

My mom used to can many years ago, and I have a quantity of canning lids left from her. She died in '73 and the lids were bought before then. Are they safe to use? I know they are relatively cheap to replace, but is there a life limit?
Denise Cline, Michigan

I probably shouldn't tell you this. Someone out there will scream. I've used my mother and mother-in-law's old lids (priced at 24¢ a box. Does that tell you something?) several times with great results. The rubber compound on the lids is thicker than modern lids, and the lids are actually heavier. I do make sure they boil a minute to soften the rubber compound, as it could be a bit hard from long storage. Don't use any with cracks or crumbly rubber compound, however.

Tattler lids

Thanks to the letter from a reader about Tattler lids and your evaluation article later, I bought a bunch of them for myself, for gifts, and to have in stock. A reusable lid is a tremendous boon to self-sufficient people, and it saves having a pallet load of one time use lids!

I have started canning with the Tattler lids. I mark on the lid each time I use it to evaluate multiple uses. First time use — 100% seal. I wash and dry lids and rings (rubber) and keep them paired for more consistency in evaluation. On the second use I had 20% no seal. This was very disturbing.

Have you had this problem and if so how did you solve it? And do you have any idea about how many times the rubber ring can be used before it fails?

David Blacknall, Texas

No, I've never had trouble with Tattler lids not resealing on subsequent uses! When I first used them, testing them out, I reused the lids many times on different foods, from walnuts to chili, canned hamburger, carrots, and spaghetti sauce. I had none fail. The rubbers can be used until they finally get dry and brittle … years and years, provided that they are kept in a relatively dark, cool place. Be sure you simmer your rubbers before putting them on the lids to soften them. And remember to follow the directions when tightening the rings prior to processing (tighten, then loosen a bit) and then tightening them after processing. I forgot this on first use and had a few not seal.

Storing canning jar flats

I know you get lots of letters so let me just say I'm a big fan of your articles … it is because of you I found Backwoods Home Magazine.

I found a really good sale on canning jar flats with the rubber around the edge. What would be the best way to store them? How long can you keep them before the rubber begins to ruin?

Bonnie Summerlin, Oklahoma

I always buy my jar lids in case lots when they're on a great sale; it's the way to go. As long as you keep the lids where it is reasonably moderate temperature and dry, they'll stay good indefinitely. I've used some that were years old. With the old lids, just be sure to keep them in hot but not boiling water for a while before you use them to soften the seal. Good for you!

Rusty canning jars

A friend gave me a lot of canning jars of all sizes (great friend). Some of them have rust and I have tried baking soda and vinegar and plain bleach to clean them and it still won't come off. Am I doomed to lose these or is there something else I can try?

Joyce Pierce, Alabama

Try the product "Iron-Out," available at most grocery stores.

Tightening lids

Love BHM *and especially your column. I have learned a lot. One item I see repeated is to tighten canning lids before pressure canning. I had always heard to leave them loose so the jars won't explode, however I do lose liquid in my jars. You have more experience by far than me and I just needed to know how tight and/or do you have any problems with breakage?*

As my mother was a "city girl," my late mother-in-law, Evelyn, was very instrumental in helping me learn to can.

Pat Everly, Ohio

Unless you are using old-style zinc lids with separate rubbers or the newer reusable Tattler lids, canning jar rings should be tightened firmly tight before processing. This means turning the rings nearly as tight as you can easily, by hand. Don't use a jar wrench to tighten; this is over-doing it.

Vacuum sealers

What about using one of those vacuum sealers for mason jars to seal them? They have an attachment to do that. Is it safe?

Bill Chappell

Well, yes ... and no. The vacuum sealer would be fine to use for sealing dehydrated food in a Mason jar to keep them extra fresh. But you have to use heat (boiling water bath or pressure canner) to seal a two-part canning jar lid in order to can safe home canned food. Bacteria are so easily transferred to food that a traditional canning process must be used for any moist canned food. Again, dehydrated foods would work well, using the vacuum method.

Vacuum sealer vs. canning

Can #10 sized cans be recanned using a pump and seal hand operated vacuum sealer? Is there any danger if a large can is opened, moved into jars and then vacuum packed? Would this preserve the food?

Brian Stanfield, Missouri

DO NOT use a vacuum sealer as a substitute for canning! It is *not* a safe method except for dry foods, such as flour or dehydrated foods. I've recanned many foods, previously packed in #10 cans, either alone or in recipes by reheating them to just boiling temperature, then packing hot into hot jars and canning it like it was fresh food.

Other ways to seal jars

I was wondering if you can vacuum seal the jars that didn't seal during the process of water bathing. If water bathing is the process in the sealing of the jar, then why can't you just seal the jar after you cook the item?

Fannie Massey

I would not advise using the vacuum seal method (assuming you mean the plastic bags you vacuum seal food in) on canning jars that didn't seal during the water bath processing. First, this is untried, and potentially dangerous. You would have to let the jar cool enough to use the vacuum sealer on. In this time it is possible that some bacteria could enter the unsealed jar. Even if sealed in, the food would still spoil. I'm not saying that it probably would spoil, but I'd rather use a tried-and-true method such as eating the food right away, refrigerating the jar until I could use it, or reprocessing the jar completely, sealing it safely by a reliable, tested method.

Sometimes I am very open to experimenting new ways, but I am a picky old so-and-so about my family's food supply.

Reusing canning seals

I have a question about the seal on my canning lids. On several of the lids that I used with the hot water bath, the seals sealed perfectly, but when I removed them they look "NEW." The food or jam is fine. Have you ever reused a canning seal?

Cybele Connor, New Jersey

I would not use a "used" lid on anything canned in a pressure canner (i.e. vegetables, meat, poultry or combinations thereof). In an emergency, I *have* used "used but pristine" lids for such things as jelly, pickles, preserves; foods that will mold if the seal fails, not grow deadly bacteria. Of course, it is not a good idea to re-use lids. All canning manuals will tell you this. And I would *never* reuse a lid that I had to pry off with a can opener as it dents the lid and damages the seal.

Any lids that I have reused, I have simmered for several minutes to ensure that the gasket material on the lid is nice and soft. A good compromise is to reuse the lids, but as lids on jars of dehydrated foods, seeds, or spices. In this way, you reuse the lid, putting it to good use. But you are not depending on it to keep your home canned food fresh, tasty, and safe.

Storage

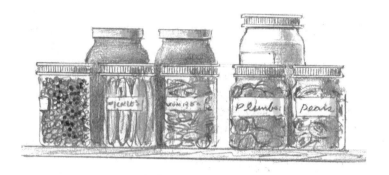

Storage of canned goods

I just got a copy of the "Emergency Preparedness and Survival Guide" from Backwoods Home Magazine *and read your chapters on food storage. I had a specific question about how long canned milk will store, but I think I should ask a more general question about storing all canned goods. If the can is opened after a long period of storage and looks and smells okay, and does not taste objectionable, would it generally be safe to consume? Thanks for your great articles. I get a lot of great and practical advice from them.*

Tom Borchers, Oregon

Yes, Tom, if your seal is good (indented firmly in the center), the food looks good, and it smells normal, it is considered safe to eat. I probably should date my own canning jars, but I don't. I can generally remember about how old a batch of food is, but not exactly. When I put my new canning on the shelves, I do take the time to pull out the oldest jars and try to stack them near the front. Then I use them first, leaving the newest produce in the back. In this way, I rotate my canned goods. But there are always some "special" foods that I kind of hoard, until I can replace them after I use a jar or two ... so they get old. But we still enjoy one of the "oldies" from time to time, as a special treat.

Stacking canned goods

In the May/June 2007 issue (Issue #105) you did an article on canning meat. I too have been canning about as long as you. However, I noticed in the pictures that you stack some of your canned goods. Is this really okay? It sure would save space but I read in a canning book years ago that by stacking the jars it could interfere with the seal. Like for some reason the seal comes undone but because of being stacked it might not show the seal is bad. Any truth to this?

Penny U'Ren, Wisconsin

I've never had a problem with a failed seal due to stacking my jars. I only stack smaller jars on top of larger ones, and never heavy ones on the top. To be absolutely safe, slip a sheet of thin plywood or masonite on top of the bottom layer; this puts pressure only on the rims of the jars, not the center. Any jars that I've had with a failed seal showed they were failed; the lid was loose, the food was nasty and smelled bad, regardless of where they were stored.

Store-canned goods are good indefinitely

We have several cases of different vegetables that are getting close to their expiration date. Is it possible to cook these up as soups and then home can them? If so, do I hot bath can or pressure can? Would I have to cook the soup or could I just warm them and then process them? What would the expected shelf life be if stored properly? Once again thanks for everything, keep up the good work and may God continue to bless you and your family.

Steve Dunn, Mississippi

I often cook up recipes from canned vegetables and tomato products that I get at outlet stores in #10 cans on a great sale. This way I have quarts and pints to deal with at meal time, not gallon cans of hominy, tomato sauce, or whatever.

Don't can up recipes just because the cans have an expiration date on them. This is bogus and causes some people to actually throw away good food! Store-canned foods are like home canned foods in this respect; once canned and properly stored, they are good almost indefinitely. True, they may lose a bit of their nutrition as this or that vitamin grows weak. But we make it up by eating plenty of home raised and wild foraged fresh food. And in a survival situation, having one can of food short of a vitamin sure beats the heck out of starving!

Yes, you can cook up soups and stews from any canned food, to re-can. You must use a pressure canner for every vegetable (except tomatoes which are a fruit … really). You must bring the food (soup or stew) up to boiling, then ladle out into hot jars. Cold or lukewarm foods are not good enough. The more foods are cooked, though, the lower the nutrition.

Shelf life of canned meats

I loved the article Jackie Clay wrote on canning meats. The question I have, though, is what is the shelf life of the canned meat?

Carol Palmer, California

The beauty of canned meat, as well as most other home canned foods, is that once properly canned and stored, they are good for years and years as long as the lid and seal are intact and good. Storing in very hot locations, places where the jars freeze in the winter, or very damp locations where the lids rust all drastically reduce the shelf life of canned foods. Ideally, you would store your jars in a relatively dark, cool, dry location that is not overly wet or humid.

Frozen canned foods

My canning jars froze, will this ruin the contents of them?

Shay Martin, Maine

No, yes, and maybe. Or maybe not. I've had frozen jars because of our move here in February of 2004. They were really frozen — for months! My pickles were toast, some of the fruit was soft, but usable in baking. Most vegetables, all of my tomato products, and meat were fine. All of the jars remained sealed. If yours are still sealed, open one at a time as you wish to use them and check out the contents. I'm thinking you may be surprised.

Shelf life of canned food

I canned many jars of food that are now about 2 years old. They look okay, but how can I tell if they are still okay to be eaten? Love your book and hope to get the next one. I am not young, almost 70, but still am very active with garden, full-time job, kids, grandkids, and great-grandkids. Am trying to instill in them country values and the need to be aware of the powers that be.

Sandra Bullock, Louisiana

Your food is perfect if the jars remain sealed, the food looks okay and smells okay. Some of my pantry food is more than 10 years old and I'm happy to break open a jar anytime!

Shelf life of home canned food

I would like to know what the shelf life is of home canned food. We have canned for some time, and our food is kept in a cool, dark, dry place.

Patrick Widner, Virginia

Well, Pat, you've hit on the very reason I home can! Your food will last nearly forever! Despite what consumer protection police say, canned food is not just good for a year. I've got 23-year-old pie cherries, canned on my pantry shelves; moose stew that is 11 years old, potatoes that are 12 years old, etc., etc. And they all look and taste perfectly fine. I'm sure they may have lost a bit of vitamins, but when combined with all the other fresh food we eat and the fact that it was home grown and put up quickly with no chemicals, we certainly don't worry about *that*.

Some fruits will soften a bit or lose color, but this does not affect their use in cobblers, pies, and other cooking. And they are more than edible.

You sure can't say that when freezing food. We only freeze food to keep large quantities while I am canning. For instance, we'll hang an elk (dressed and skinned, covered with old clean sheets) frozen in a tree, cutting off a quarter with a chainsaw (vegetable oil in oiler!), to thaw so I can home can it. That's it, for us, *period*. Once my food is in a jar, it won't freezer burn or spoil because of power outages.

More canning questions

Is canning water worth the trouble?

Some friends and I were discussing long-term water re-serve supplies. We had the idea to "can" water in large mason jars. Would we need to use a pressure canner or would a water bath be sufficient and should we boil the water first?

Also, how long would these "canned" water supplies last before they would need to be emptied and reprocessed?

J.T. Smith

Yes, you could can water, but I really think it would be more work than it would be worth. If you simply fill your jars with clean water and put the lids on without processing, the water would remain good for at least a year, providing you keep it in a cool, dark place to avoid possible algae growth.

After this time, simply pour out the "old" water and replace it with fresh. Remember that in an emergency you can boil just about any water, rendering it okay to drink. This would certainly apply to "old" water in sterile jars you forgot to rotate.

I've kept many gallon milk jugs, which I washed well with dish soap and hot water, then filled with fresh water in my basement, just in case. And this water was perfectly good after a year's storage. It does taste a bit of plastic, but in a survival situation you'd be glad to have it. Even the gallon in the back of the Suburban, in summer's heat, sure beats nothing when you're broken down way back in the woods.

If you decide to can water, remember that boiled water tastes flat. To improve the taste, open the jar to admit oxygen, then shut it and shake well. It really does help. You don't have to pressure can water. You can simply water bath it for 10 minutes. But I still think it would be extra work when there are other alternatives.

Sending canned foods through the mail a no-no

I have a son who is in the Navy and he is missing my home-cooked meals.

I was wondering if you can send cooked white beans or red beans processed in a jar, and how long it would last? He is in the states but we are in Louisiana and he is in California. I send him corn bread but I had a wild idea about sending him some cooked beans in a jar.

Julie Grivat, Louisiana

I have to laugh, because I sent my oldest son, Bill, some home canned chili, which was his favorite, through the mail. It must have had some rough handling between Montana and Minnesota because the seal came loose, and when he got it the chili reeked! The same year, I sent my oldest daughter some of her favorite bread and butter pickles, along with two pair of wool socks. The pickles, too, came unsealed, and Randie's wool socks ended up smelling like pickles … four washings later, too!

Now, we've moved around a bit, and hauled our pantry full of jars up dreadfully rocky mountain trails, across the country where they've been tossed into trucks and shoved around roughly. Very few ever came unsealed, but all of my mailed foods did. What does that say for the Postal Service? And United Parcel is no better.

If you want to send your son something tasty from home, better to choose homemade candy, cookies, bars, jam, or jelly. The rest don't seem to make it.

Using salt in canning

My husband needs to watch his sodium intake. I'd like to can some beef cubes, and the recipe I have calls for ½ teaspoon salt per pint. Can I halve that, or even omit it altogether?

Julie Hamilton, Pennsylvania

Good news! You don't need to put salt into anything you can. The "add ½ tsp salt" directions are only for taste enhancement. It does nothing to keep the food good. This goes for meat, vegetables, and poultry. You *do* need to use it for pickle recipes, but you can choose ones with less salt in the recipes to help.

81

Is adding salt necessary?

I personally have been canning foods for maybe 27 years now. I no longer use a water bath canner because I don't have the touch needed to make good jams and jellies and I hate adding all the heat to the kitchen when making tomato sauce (okay — thick juice really). I use the pressure canner because it is reasonably quick and economical and I feel the food is safe when it comes out and the seal holds. I have never hesitated to use something I canned to feed family or friends (again, as long as the seal is intact), especially since the night we had a party and a guest (surgeon) looked over the canned deer and chicken, asked how I processed it, and then admitted she didn't even go to those lengths to sterilize her surgical instruments! Ouch!

I am, however, confused by the constant instruction to add salt. So much per pint, so much per quart. Is this really a safety issue? Is a jar of meat canned at 10-15 lbs. pressure (hard to control in a canner with a dial, easy with a jiggle weight) for up to 90-100 minutes any safer if I throw in a little salt?

This salt thing goes back to my earliest canning guide (1940s) and up to the latest "Ball Blue Book" on my shelf. Blood pressure and heart disease run rampant in my family and I have always hoped to go easy on the salt I add but I don't want to lose any edge I may have in safe food prep.

Greg Pitaniello, West Virginia

Salt has absolutely nothing to do with the safety or preservation of canned food. Salt is added solely for taste enhancement. If you don't want to add it to your food, you don't need to. Period. Now isn't that good news?

But I'm sorry to hear that you've given up on your water bath canner. Bummer! If I can make jams and jellies, anyone can. Especially if you use added commercial pectin and follow the directions. Most folks have failures in this department from doubling or tripling the recipe. It often doesn't jell like it should. And no tomato sauce? Whew, I'm feeling faint. So cook it down outside, on the grill. I made tomato sauce in New Mexico and never felt particularly overheated. Of course, I did it in the early morning, when the heat hadn't gotten bad yet or during a rainy spell when I didn't notice the added heat.

I do "cheat," though, by using a tomato strainer, which removes the skins and seeds, so I don't have all that boiling water to skin the tomatoes first. I just cook down the thick purée. And by using a meaty variety of tomato, this really doesn't take so long.

Calcium in water

My question concerns calcium in my water. Our well water tastes great, and is safe, yet there are calcium deposits in our pans. Filtering does not remove the calcium. When I boil water to use for sterilizing jars, they all have calcium deposits on the glass, and the lids and rings are also affected. I know I can clean off the outside of the jar, but sometimes I even need vinegar to help. How does this calcium affect the canning process: in the canners, in the jars and with the recipes?

Sue Corbin, Minnesota

Usually, calcium does not greatly affect the canning process. You can usually be rid of the deposit on your jars by adding about ¼ cup of vinegar to the water you use for sterilizing jars. The one problem some people have with canning with calcium in the water is pickling. If you don't have any problems, great. If you seem to be having soft or discolored pickles, use bottled water for your pickling.

Hard water

I got a new pressure canner not too long ago. We have very heavy water and the canner is aluminum. Can I add some vinegar to the water in the canner to stop the scale?

Jo Ann Nelson, California

Yes, you can add a little vinegar to your canner. But you probably would find it easier to just use some soft water, such as rainwater, spring water, or water from a friend's house for your pressure canning, as you really don't use too much at a time.

Old vinegar

I just found a gallon jug of white vinegar dated 8-9-99! Could I still use this for canning or should I just put it with the cleaning supplies?

Sandra Agostini, Missouri

I've never had vinegar go bad during storage. Take a good look at it, then when you open it, give it a sniff. If it looks good and smells normal, I'd go ahead and use it.

Cold pack

I have come across several canning recipes that say things like, "cold pack the soup for an hour." Could you explain please?

Donna Shepherd, California

The term "cold pack" usually means process in a boiling water bath canner. *Don't* do it! The only safe way to can any meat, poultry, or vegetable-based soup is to pressure can it.

Some people confuse the term "cold pack" with "raw pack." You can raw pack many foods that then are pressure canned. This just means you pack raw food in the jar with no pre-cooking.

Pantry, salt, and oven canning

I have seen the pictures of your well stocked pantry. Good for you. The only thing that I see that you need is some removable boards across the front because of the possibility of an earth tremor or earthquake.

Have you ever used the salt that people put into their swimming pools in your canning? It says on the 40 lb. package that it is food grade. It is 40 lbs. for $14.02.

My cousin (68 years old) cans tomatoes, okra, etc. by cooking almost fully on the stove and then putting the quart jars in the oven for one hour at 200°F (should be 250°F).

David Dawson, Texas

The reason I don't use earthquake protection in my pantry is that there have only been six incidences of earthquake tremors in Minnesota's recorded history, and none caused more than barely-felt tremors anywhere in Minnesota. You plan for the most possible emergencies, but never can plan for them all.

No, I don't use pool salt for pickling or canning. It probably is safe; I know about the food grade label, but it also says "not for human consumption." It's probably a legality in this sue-happy world, but for the amount of salt I use every year, I'm not going to switch.

Your cousin is playing with fire with his oven canning. This method is not safe, especially with okra, no matter if he boils it first or at what temperature he uses in the oven. Oven canning does not circulate heat around and through the jars as does boiling water. (Okra is a low-acid vegetable and *must* be pressure canned.)

Other titles available from
Backwoods Home Publications

The Best of the First Two Years
A Backwoods Home Anthology—The Third Year
A Backwoods Home Anthology—The Fourth Year
A Backwoods Home Anthology—The Fifth Year
A Backwoods Home Anthology—The Sixth Year
A Backwoods Home Anthology—The Seventh Year
A Backwoods Home Anthology—The Eighth Year
A Backwoods Home Anthology—The Ninth Year
A Backwoods Home Anthology—The Tenth Year
A Backwoods Home Anthology—The Eleventh Year
A Backwoods Home Anthology—The Twelfth Year
A Backwoods Home Anthology—The Thirteenth Year
A Backwoods Home Anthology—The Fourteenth Year
A Backwoods Home Anthology—The Fifteenth Year
A Backwoods Home Anthology—The Sixteenth Year
A Backwoods Home Anthology—The Seventeenth Year
A Backwoods Home Anthology—The Eighteenth Year
A Backwoods Home Anthology—The Nineteenth Year
A Backwoods Home Anthology—The Twentieth Year
A Backwoods Home Anthology—The Twenty-first Year
A Backwoods Home Anthology—The Twenty-second Year
A Backwoods Home Anthology—The Twenty-third Year
A Backwoods Home Anthology—The Twenty-fourth Year
A Backwoods Home Anthology—The Twenty-fifth Year
A Backwoods Home Anthology—The Twenty-sixth Year
A Backwoods Home Anthology—The Twenty-seventh Year
A Backwoods Home Anthology—The Twenty-eighth Year
A Backwoods Home Anthology—The Twenty-ninth Year